SCOTLAND

What do you think of when you hear the name 'Scotland'? Golf? Tartan? Bagpipes? The Loch Ness Monster? These are all part of Scotland – but there is much more too.

There are old castles and exciting new buildings. There are beautiful queens, brave kings – and a very famous James Bond. There are cities with great shops and museums, and quiet islands where you see nobody all day. There are long, long summer days, and in the middle of winter, when the days are short and dark, one of the biggest street parties in the world! Welcome to a very special country . . .

OXFORD BOOKWORMS LIBRARY

Factfiles

Scotland

Stage 1 (400 headwords)

Factfiles Series Editor: Christine Lindop

STEVE FLINDERS

Scotland

OXFORD UNIVERSITY PRESS

OXFORD
UNIVERSITY PRESS

Great Clarendon Street, Oxford OX2 6DP

Oxford University Press is a department of the University of Oxford.
It furthers the University's objective of excellence in research, scholarship,
and education by publishing worldwide in

Oxford New York

Auckland Cape Town Dar es Salaam Hong Kong Karachi
Kuala Lumpur Madrid Melbourne Mexico City Nairobi
New Delhi Shanghai Taipei Toronto

With offices in

Argentina Austria Brazil Chile Czech Republic France Greece
Guatemala Hungary Italy Japan Poland Portugal Singapore
South Korea Switzerland Thailand Turkey Ukraine Vietnam

OXFORD and OXFORD ENGLISH are registered trade marks of
Oxford University Press in the UK and in certain other countries

ISBN: 978 0 19 423623 2

A complete recording of this Bookworms edition of *Scotland*
is available in a CD pack ISBN 978 0 19 423626 3

Printed in China

Word count (main text): 5,150

For more information on the Oxford Bookworms Library,
visit www.oup.com/bookworms

ACKNOWLEDGEMENTS
Illustration page 4 by Peter Bull

The publishers would like to thank the following for permission to reproduce images:

Alamy Images pp10 (Tartan kilts/Peter Scholey), 14 (Tearoom/Neil McAllister), 15 (Aberdeen Harbour/
David Robertson), 18 (Steam train/Blackout Concepts), 19 (Heather/David Boag), 21 (Callanish Standing
Stones/nagelestock.com), 23 (White water kayaking/Arch White), 27 (Old Bess prototype steam engine/
The Print Collector), 28 (Sherlock Holmes/Pictorial Press Ltd), 29 (Bread/avatra images), 31 (Desserts/
Simon Reddy), 35 (The Carnegie Library of Pittsburgh/Andre Jenny); Bridgeman Art Library Ltd pp27
(James Watt (1736-1819), after William Beechey (1753-1839), Partridge, John (1790-1872) / Scottish
National Portrait Gallery, Edinburgh, Scotland), 33 (Lochaber No More, 1883, Nicol, John Watson/© The
Fleming-Wyfold Art Foundation); Cephas Picture Library p32 (Whisky distillery/Joris Luyten); FLPA p19
(Red deer/Desmond Dugan); Getty Images pp2 (Offshore drilling rigs/Jason Hawkes/Riser), 3 (Hadrian's
Wall/Adam Woolfitt/Robert Harding World Imagery), 6 (Mary Stuart (1542-87)/Francois Clouet/The
Bridgeman Art Library), 9 (Edinburgh Castle/Kathy Collins/Taxi), 12 (White Star liner Queen Mary/
Hulton Archive), 14 (Rangers football supporters/AFP), 20 (Fingal's Cave/Jim Richardson/National
Geographic), 34 (Emigrants at Glasgow docks/Hulton Archive), 35 (Tartan Day Parade), 38 (Scottish
Parliament Debating Chamber/Kathy Collins/Photographer's Choice); OUP pp43 (Glencoe, Scotland/
Digital Vision), 43 (Tartan/Corel), 43 (Mattiscombe Beach/Corel), 43 (The Round Tower in Windsor), 43
(Lake District/Digital Vision), 43 (Buck Island/Photodisc); Photolibrary p26 (Haggis ceremony/Anthony
Blake/Fresh Food Images); PunchStock p16 (Loch Ness/Photodisc); Rex Features pp8 (The abandoned
village Riasg Buidhe/Design Pics Inc), 36 (Sean Connery/James Fraser); Scottish Viewpoint pp (Eilean
Donan Castle/Colin Paterson/www.scottishviewpoint.com), 11 (Edinburgh Military Tattoo), 22
(St Andrews golf course), 24 (Highland Games), 25 (Charlotte Square), 30 (Scottish fish); The Royal
Collection Picture Library p7 (The Battle of Culloden/The Royal Collection © 2009 Her Majesty Queen
Elizabeth II).

2001815
17.50

CONTENTS

1 A special country

There is nowhere like Scotland.

Scotland is a country in a country. It is part of Great Britain (England, Scotland, and Wales), and of the United Kingdom (England, Scotland, Wales, and Northern Ireland).

Scotland is in the far north-west of Europe, between the Atlantic Ocean and the North Sea. It is often cold and grey, and it rains a lot in some parts of the country. But the people of Scotland love their country, and many visitors to Scotland love it too. They love the beautiful hills and mountains of the north, the sea and the 800 islands, and the six cities – Edinburgh, Glasgow, Aberdeen, Dundee, Inverness, and Stirling. The country is special and Scottish people are special too: often warm and friendly.

There are about five million people in Scotland. Most Scots live in the south, in or near the big cities of Edinburgh and Glasgow. Most of the north of the country is very empty; not many people live there.

A Scottish person is also called a Scot, but you *cannot* talk about a Scotch person: Scotch means whisky, a drink made in Scotland. Scottish people are British, because Scotland is part of Great Britain, but you must not call Scottish people English! The Scots and the English are different.

Looking for oil

These days everyone in Scotland speaks English, but at one time, people in the north and west of Scotland did not speak English. They had a different language, a beautiful language called Gaelic. About 60,000 people – 1 per cent of the people in Scotland – speak Gaelic now. But many more want Gaelic in their lives because it is part of the story of Scotland.

Scotland is not a very hot country. In the summer the days are long and it can be warm. But in the winter the days can be just seven hours long, and it often rains.

For many years, Scotland was a poor country, but now things are better for most people. There is oil and gas in the sea between Scotland and Norway. Edinburgh is an important place for money, and there are big banks there like the Royal Bank of Scotland. People in many countries drink Scotch whisky, and the whisky business makes a lot of money for Scotland. Tourists visit this beautiful country and that brings money to Scotland too. Many people love living and working there, and more than 20 million visitors go to Scotland each year.

2 Scotland's past

Scotland is the oldest country in the world. Why? Because the hills of the north-west and the Hebridean islands are more than 2,700 million years old. You can walk on some of the oldest rocks in the world there.

People first lived there 9,000 years ago. At Skara Brae on the Orkney Islands, in the far north of Scotland, you can see the houses of early people from about five thousand years ago. The houses at Knap of Howar, also on the Orkneys, are the oldest in Europe.

The Romans went to Scotland, but they did not stay there for long. Between AD 122 and 128 they built Hadrian's Wall. It was 117 kilometres long, and went from sea to sea across the most northern part of England. The Romans stayed in England for nearly three hundred years until about AD 400, and then they left and went back to Rome. Today you can visit Hadrian's Wall in the north of England and walk along parts of it.

Hadrian's Wall

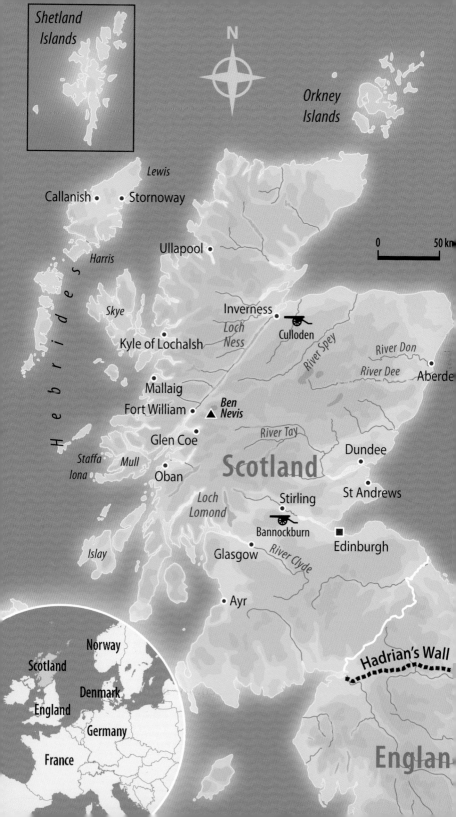

Who were the first Scots? The people north of Hadrian's Wall were called Picts by the Romans. We can still see some of their story in their pictures in stone. But there were also Scotti from Ireland (the name 'Scotland' comes from the Scotti), Vikings from Norway, and some English people from the south. These different peoples came under one king in the 800s. The first king of all the Scots, many people say, was Kenneth MacAlpin. He was king from 843 to 858. But the most famous Scottish king of this early time is Macbeth (1040–1057). He is famous because Shakespeare wrote about him. For Shakespeare, Macbeth was a very bad man – but he was not worse than many other kings of those early days.

There were many battles between England and Scotland. One important Scot was William Wallace (about 1270–1305). You can learn about him in the film *Braveheart*. Then in 1314, the Scottish King Robert the Bruce took his men to the Battle of Bannockburn. After the battle, 10,000 Englishmen were dead, and Robert became one of the most important kings in the story of Scotland. Soon after, Scotland was free and stayed free for nearly three hundred years.

In 1542, a little girl called Mary became queen of Scotland: she was six days old, and only the second woman to be queen of this country. Mary Queen of Scots became a tall and beautiful woman, but some Scots did not want her to be queen. Mary went to England and asked Elizabeth, the English queen, for help, but she did not get it. She never returned to Scotland, and died in England after nineteen years. You can read Mary's story

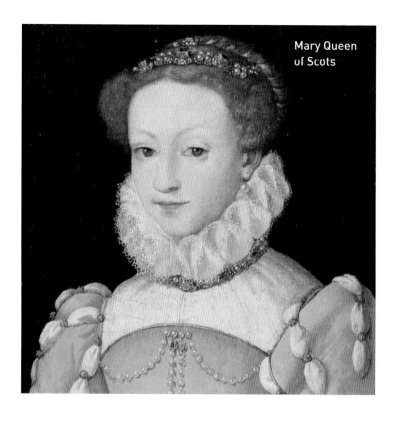

Mary Queen of Scots

in *Mary, Queen of Scots* (Oxford Bookworms Stage 1). Mary's son James Stuart became king of Scotland and then King James the First of England too. In 1707, the two countries became Great Britain.

In the 1700s, Scotland was more like two countries than one: there were rich cities in the south, but there were poor country people in the Highlands (the hill country in the centre and the north of Scotland). At that time, Edinburgh was one of the most important cities in Europe and many famous thinkers lived there. Then in the 1800s Glasgow became rich; people built big ships there, and later trains. So the south of Scotland had busy cities with beautiful buildings, lots of work, and money.

In the Highlands, things were very different. After 1714, Great Britain had German kings, from Hanover in north Germany. Many Scots in the Highlands wanted a Scottish king – someone from the Stuart family like Mary and James, not a German king in London. They wanted Charles Stuart – 'Bonnie Prince Charlie' – the grandson of the last Stuart king, James the Second of England and the Seventh of Scotland. Charles Stuart left France and came to Scotland: he wanted to be King of Scotland and England too. But Charles and his men lost the Battle of Culloden, near Inverness, in 1746. Culloden was the last big battle in Great Britain.

The Battle of Culloden

After the battle, the British soldiers looked for Charles, but he went into the hills. The people of the Highlands and the islands helped him to go back to France, but life became difficult for them after that. The British soldiers stayed in the Highlands, and took away houses and land from the friends of Charles Stuart. After this many poor families left the Highlands and went to the cities in the south of Scotland, or to other countries – the USA, Canada, Australia, and New Zealand. Some went because they wanted to begin a new life, but others went because the rich owners of the land in Scotland wanted to put animals there. Between 1840 and 1880, 40,000 people left just one island – the island of Skye.

Life became more difficult in the 1900s, but oil and gas in the North Sea began to bring money to Scotland again in the 1970s. Let's look now at some of the famous places in the Scotland of today.

Houses left in the Highlands

3 Edinburgh

Many people begin a visit to Scotland in Edinburgh, the capital city. Edinburgh is an old city with many important and interesting buildings, and about 470,000 people live there. After London, Edinburgh is the second city for visitors in Britain.

Come to Edinburgh by train from the south, and you arrive at Waverley Station. When you come out of the station, Edinburgh Castle is in front of you, high up on

a hill. From the castle, you can see all over the city. You can see the famous One O'Clock Gun – and at 1 o'clock, from Monday to Saturday, you can hear it too. It makes a very big noise!

Edinburgh is built on hills, but you can walk around the city easily. From the castle, you can go down the Royal Mile to Holyroodhouse. This building, three hundred years old, is the home of Queen Elizabeth the Second when she comes to Edinburgh. This part of the city is called 'the Old Town'.

Then take a walk along Princes Street in 'the New Town'. The New Town (1767–1840) is more than 150 years old now but still has this name. Some shops have the famous Scottish tartans. Each clan – a big, old Scottish family is called a clan – has its own tartan, and in the windows you can see the different tartans for famous Scottish clans. People with a Scottish family name can buy and wear the family tartan. (People without a Scottish name can buy and wear a tartan too!)

Tartan kilts

Edinburgh
Military Tattoo

Edinburgh has many wonderful things. The buildings in the New Town – in Charlotte Square, for example – are very beautiful. There are very good museums: the National Museum of Scotland is near the Royal Mile, and tells you a lot about the Scotland of yesterday and today. The National Gallery of Scotland, near the castle, has beautiful pictures from Scotland and from many other countries too.

In August, thousands of people come to the Edinburgh Festival. Singing, dancing, cinema, books, pictures, theatre – you can see and do hundreds of different things at the festival. And also in August, every evening for three weeks, you can go to the Edinburgh Military Tattoo at Edinburgh Castle. There you can see soldiers and hear music from Scotland and from lots of other countries.

On 31 December everyone wants to be in the city centre for the famous street party for Hogmanay – that is the Scottish name for New Year's Eve. But there are only 100,000 tickets, and they go very quickly! The party begins in one year and finishes in the next – that *is* a good time!

4 Glasgow

Glasgow is Scotland's biggest city and the third biggest in the United Kingdom after London and Birmingham. About 630,000 people live in the city and about 1.2 million in and near it. It is not very far from Edinburgh – about fifty minutes by train – but it is very different.

The River Clyde runs through the centre of Glasgow, and it has an important part in the story of Glasgow. Two hundred years ago, Glasgow was a small town. Then, British ships began to go all over the world. Big ships came up and down the River Clyde. They carried things from other countries. In the 1800s, Britain was the richest country in the world. Shipbuilding became very important and Glasgow became a city of shipbuilders. At one time it

Glasgow, 1936

was the fourth largest city in Europe after London, Paris, and Berlin. You can see some of the beautiful buildings from that time in George Square. Today there is not much shipbuilding; some parts of Glasgow are very poor and many people have no work. But things are changing in Glasgow. Ask a Glaswegian (a person from Glasgow). To them, Glasgow is the friendliest city in Britain, and one of the most exciting cities in Britain too.

There are lots of things to do at night in Glasgow. It is perhaps the best city in Britain after London for shopping too. Like Edinburgh, it is a green city. It has seventy parks, and you can often see the hills from the centre of the city.

It is a city of museums. You can see many beautiful pictures in the Glasgow City Museum and Art Gallery, and in the Burrell Collection and Pollok House, south of the Clyde.

Willow Tea Rooms

It is the city of Charles Rennie Mackintosh. About a hundred years ago Mackintosh and three friends began a new look in building: art nouveau. Much of Mackintosh's best work is in Glasgow. His Glasgow School of Art is on Renfrew Street. After you visit it, you can have a coffee at the Willow Tea Rooms, also by Mackintosh, on Sauchiehall Street.

And Glasgow is, of course, a big football city. You can watch Glasgow Celtic at Celtic Park, or Glasgow Rangers at the Ibrox Stadium, on Saturdays between August and May.

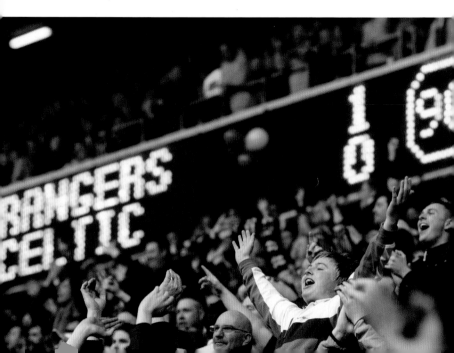

5   Four Scottish cities

Aberdeen, with 192,000 people, is the third biggest city in Scotland. It is in the east of the country, on the North Sea, and it is between two rivers – the Dee and the Don. Fishing and shipbuilding were once important here, but now it is famous as the oil capital of the UK. Boats and planes leave Aberdeen every day for the oil and gas fields of the North Sea. It has two universities, and many wonderful parks and gardens. The musicians Annie Lennox and Evelyn Glennie both come from Aberdeen.

Aberdeen

Visitors to Aberdeen often go to its beautiful long beach, or go climbing south of the city. Aberdeen is close to the cold and beautiful mountains called the Cairngorms, and there are more than 350 castles in this part of the country. One of them is Balmoral, the queen's castle. Queen Elizabeth comes here every summer.

Dundee, on the River Tay, is near the North Sea too. Like Glasgow and Aberdeen, it was once important for shipbuilding. The ship *Discovery* was built here, and left Dundee in 1901 for Antarctica. Now, more than a hundred years later, the ship is back in Dundee again, and you can visit it there. Dundee is also famous for . . . marmalade! The Keiller family began making orange marmalade here in 1797, and it became famous all over the world.

Loch Ness

Inverness is the only city in the Highlands. The best bagpipers in the world come here to play every September. It is close to the beautiful lake called Loch Ness (loch is the Gaelic word for 'lake'). A very big animal called the Loch Ness Monster, or Nessie, lives in Loch Ness. An old story says this, and thousands of tourists go there every year to look for it. But Nessie does not come. Perhaps this is just a story for tourists.

Then there is Stirling, to the north-east of Glasgow. Many visitors go through Stirling when they go to the Highlands. It has a wonderful castle, one of the biggest and most important castles in Scotland. The battle of Bannockburn in 1314 was near here, and here Mary became queen of Scotland when she was only six days old.

6 Highlands and islands

Highlands

The Highlands, in the north and west of Scotland, are a special part of the world. There are not a lot of people here – only eight people per square kilometre – but there is a lot of beautiful country, with lochs, rivers, and hills. The Highlands have two of the most wonderful train journeys in the world: from Inverness to Kyle of Lochalsh, and from Fort William to Mallaig. Or visitors can go by road past the beautiful Loch Lomond to the mountains at Glen Coe.

Do you love to be out of the cities, walking, climbing, looking for birds and animals, or taking photos? Then the Highlands are for you. The mountains are not very high – Ben Nevis, the highest in the UK, is 1,344 metres – but they can be difficult. Sometimes cold weather comes from the north, so walkers and climbers need to be careful in the winter, and in the summer too.

What can you see in the Highlands? There are not many trees on the hills, but there is beautiful heather. The water in the lochs is cold and dark. Red deer run across the hills, and perhaps you can see golden eagles high up in the sky. When you leave the road, you are soon in empty country; there is nothing but the hills and the sky, the birds and the animals.

Heather

Red deer

Islands

Scotland has hundreds of islands, and life is different there. The island towns are small. On some islands, like Skye and the islands of the Hebrides, many of the people speak Gaelic. On the islands of Lewis and Harris, some people do not work, drive, or watch TV on Sundays. In the north, the islands of Orkney and Shetland are nearer to Norway than to London.

Fingal's cave, Isle of Staffa

From Oban in the west of Scotland you can go to some of the islands in the Inner Hebrides. Here you can see sea animals like seals. From Mull you can go to see the beautiful caves of Staffa, or you can visit Iona. Saint Columba came to the small island of Iona from Ireland in 563, and began to teach people about Christianity. Today Iona is an important Christian centre and half a million people go there every year. The bodies of Kenneth MacAlpin and other Scottish kings are here on Iona. You can also go to Skye, perhaps the most famous and the most beautiful of the islands of Scotland, and see the dark mountains called the Cuillin near the sea.

From Ullapool, you can go across to Lewis in the Outer Hebrides. There are long, white, empty beaches here and the 5,000-year-old stone circle at Callanish. There are fifty standing stones at Callanish. Time goes more slowly in this quiet, special place.

Callanish standing stones

7 Sport and free time

Many Scottish people love sport, and in Scotland many people play golf – the rich and the not so rich. Golf began in this country, and the golf capital of Scotland is St Andrews, a small university city near Edinburgh. There are more than four hundred golf courses in Scotland, and many of them are very beautiful. In the summer, when the days are long, you can play from seven in the morning to ten at night.

St Andrew's golf course

Football is also very important: in 2006 Scotland had the tenth highest number of football clubs of any country in the world. Celtic and Rangers are the biggest and the most famous Scottish clubs but others like Aberdeen also do well in Scotland and in Europe. The Scots play rugby football too, and it is an important sport in Scotland. In 1990 Scotland beat England, Wales, Ireland, and France at rugby – and every year the Scots want to do this again! But now Italy plays too, so they need to beat five countries, not four.

Scotland's hills and mountains are good for sports too – walking, climbing, cycling, and more. And there are lots of exciting sports on, in, and under the water, in the lochs, rivers, and the sea. You can take a kayak down a fast river, for example, or out to sea. The rain does not matter when you do these sports!

Between May and September, in more than a hundred different places in Scotland, people meet at a Highland Games – a festival of Scottish sports and music. You can see big men tossing the caber, listen to Scottish music on the bagpipes, and watch Scottish dancing.

Not all Scots men have kilts, but more and more of them wear one sometimes, and lots of people wear kilts to the Games. When a Scotsman wears a kilt, he is saying, 'I like being Scottish.' A kilt needs about six metres of tartan. When one of the big clans – like Clan Donald, Mackenzie, or Stewart – has a

Kayaking

Tossing the caber

big meeting, people come from many countries. Many of them wear kilts in the clan tartan when they come. One clan in the USA – Clan Donald – has 4,000 families. Their families went from Scotland to the USA perhaps 150 years ago, but they still want to be Scottish.

8   Five great Scots

Scotland is not a big country and does not have many people, but there are many famous and important Scots. Here are five of them.

Robert Adam (1728–1792) made some of the best buildings in Great Britain in the second half of the 1700s. He went to school and university in Edinburgh, and then to Rome for five years to learn about the buildings there. Then he came back to Britain. He worked on the New Town in Edinburgh and you can see buildings by him in Charlotte Square. There are many beautiful buildings by Adam in England and Scotland. People come from all over Europe and America to look at them.

Charlotte Square

Haggis on Burns Night

David Hume (1711–1776) was a great thinker and writer. People still read and talk about his books today because they are so important. He also wrote a very long *History of England* – at that time, the most important book of this kind. Hume went to the University of Edinburgh when he was twelve years old. Later he went to France and made friends with famous French thinkers like Voltaire and Rousseau. His most important book is *A Treatise of Human Nature* (1739–1740).

The next great Scot is Robert Burns (1759–1796); the Scots call him Robbie or Rabbie Burns. He was born into a poor country family, the oldest of seven children, near Ayr in south-west Scotland. He began writing poems when he was still a boy. He wrote about important things – about life and love, rich people and poor people, and Scotland. His words still speak to us today and many Scots love his poems.

Burns was born on 25 January, and that night is called Burns Night by the Scots. On Burns Night there are special dinners not just in Scotland but for Scottish people in other countries too. They eat haggis (a special

Scottish food), drink whisky, and say poems by Burns. And at midnight on 31 December in many English-speaking countries, people sing the words of Burns when they sing 'Auld Lang Syne' (the name of the song means something like 'long long ago').

James Watt (1736–1819) was born in Greenock near Glasgow and did not often go to school when he was a child: he stayed at home and his mother was his teacher. Watt was a quick thinker and he liked to build things with his hands. He got work building things for the teachers at the University of Glasgow. There he became interested in steam engines. He began a business with his friend Matthew Boulton, and from 1794 to 1824 they made 1,164 steam engines. These engines changed Great Britain and the world. After Watt, the world was a different place.

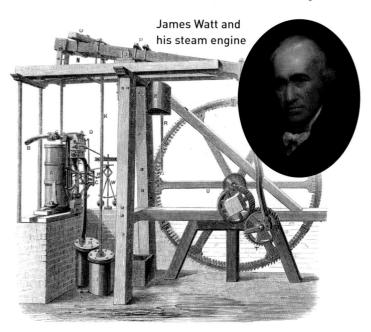

James Watt and his steam engine

Sir Arthur Conan Doyle (1859–1930) was born in Edinburgh, went to the University of Edinburgh, and became a doctor. But he did not make much money as a doctor so he began to write stories about a detective called Sherlock Holmes. Soon Sherlock Holmes was famous and Conan Doyle became rich and famous too. He wrote many stories about Holmes and his friend Dr Watson, and also wrote stories about a man called Professor Challenger.

Sherlock Holmes

There are films of many Sherlock Holmes stories, and you can read some of them in Bookworms: *Sherlock Holmes and the Duke's Son* and *Sherlock Holmes and the Sport of Kings* (Oxford Bookworms Stage 1).

Do you know any other great Scots?

9 Food and drink

Food In the earliest days Scottish people took their food from the sea, the rivers, and the land. From the sea and the rivers came fish, and from the land they got fruit, vegetables, and meat. And they got oats from the land too. They made their bread from oats, and they made porridge from oats and water for a hot breakfast.

Oats and oat bread

People still eat all of these things in Scotland today, but they eat new things too. From 1900 on, many people began to come to Scotland from countries like Italy and India, and they brought different food with them.

There is a lot of good food in Scotland. It is famous for its fish, like salmon and haddock, and for other food from the sea. Fish farming is very important for Scotland; it gives work to about 6,000 people, and brings lots of money into the country. Then there is Scottish beef – the best beef in the world, the Scots say – and haggis, made from meat, oats, and other things. Scottish raspberries are also very good; the Scots like to make a dish called cranachan with raspberries, oats, and whisky. People with lots of money can go to a hotel like Gleneagles, near Perth – perhaps the most famous hotel in Scotland today. It has 232 bedrooms, three golf courses – and some of the best Scottish food.

Fish and seafood

But good food is not a part of life for everybody in Scotland, and some poorer Scots do not eat very well. British men usually live to seventy-seven years old, but in some parts of Glasgow they only live to fifty-four. Better food is very important for Scottish people today and tomorrow.

Cranachan and raspberries

Drink The word 'whisky' comes from the Gaelic 'uisge-beatha' – the water of life. Whisky – also called 'Scotch' – is made in a distillery. There are more than one hundred distilleries in Scotland – some near Edinburgh and Glasgow in the south, one on the island of Skye, and three on the Orkneys in the north. There are nine on the small island of Islay. About half of the distilleries are near the River Spey, east of Inverness; many visitors like to visit the distilleries there and try the different whiskies. Visitors to Edinburgh can visit the Scotch Whisky Heritage Centre near the castle.

Scotch whisky

Whisky is good but another drink in Scotland is better: water. The whisky is good because the water from the hills is good. On a hot day, a drink of Scottish hill water can be the best drink in the world.

10 Scotland and the world

Scotland is a small country. Only five million people live there. But for millions more across the world, Scotland is very important. Why is this?

In the 1800s many people left Scotland and went to other countries. People in the Highlands left their homes and villages because they were very poor and hungry.

Leaving Scotland

Leaving for Canada, 1923

Sometimes the rich people there wanted them to leave. Many others from the south of Scotland left because they wanted a better life in a new country. Between the 1820s and 1914, more than two million people went from Scotland across the seas to the United States, Canada, Australia, and New Zealand. More went in the 1920s. Today there are six million Scottish Americans in the USA. Every year many people walk through New York on 6 April – Tartan Day. A lot of Scottish Americans go back to Scotland as tourists. They want to find their past and to understand it.

So Scotland is important in the story of other countries too. Two great Scots in the USA are Alexander Graham Bell (1847–1922) and Andrew Carnegie (1837–1919). Bell made the first telephone. He began the Bell Telephone Company in 1877, and by 1885 more than 150,000 people

in the USA had telephones. In 1915 he made the first telephone call across the United States from New York to San Francisco. After he died in Canada, at the age of seventy-five, all the telephones in North America were quiet for one minute to remember him.

Andrew Carnegie's family left Scotland when he was eleven and went to the USA. Carnegie worked hard, and by the 1880s he had many businesses and was very rich – the richest man in the world. When he stopped working, he gave his money to other people. Carnegie's money built schools,

Tartan Day, New York

universities, and other buildings in the USA, the UK,
Australia, New Zealand, and Ireland. Today his money
still helps millions of people around the world every
year.

Many Scots love to visit other countries and do new
things. David Livingstone (1813–1873) went to Africa to
begin schools and to tell Africans about Christianity. He
was the first European to see the Victoria Falls, between

Zambia and Zimbabwe, and the first to go across Africa from the Atlantic in the west to the Indian Ocean in the east. Alan Bean (1932–) is a Scottish American. When he went to the moon in 1969 – only the fourth man to walk on the moon – he took some tartan with him. Scots like to go to new places!

Sean Connery

Who is the most famous Scot in the world today? To many people it is the film star Sean Connery (1930–). Sean Connery did a lot of different jobs before he began working in television and cinema. Then in 1962 he was James Bond in the first James Bond film, *Dr No*. After this he was famous everywhere. He made six more James Bond films, and made many other films after that. To many people, his best film is *The Untouchables* (1987). Connery does not make films now and does not live in Scotland, but he loves Scotland very much and does not want it to be part of the United Kingdom.

11 Scotland today and tomorrow

The story of Scotland is interesting and sometimes exciting, but it is not an easy story. Some Scots, like Sean Connery, want Scotland to be just Scotland, and not part of the United Kingdom.

Scotland is still a country of rich and poor. The past is important, but many Scots also want to think about Scotland today and tomorrow. The Scots in the USA, Australia, Canada, and New Zealand love the old things – the music, the dancing, the tartans. But many of the Scots in Scotland want their country to look to the future, not the past. Scotland, they say, can be like Norway – a country with five million people and with a lot of money from oil. Scotland has money from oil, fish farming, visits from tourists, banks, computers, and many other businesses. And there is new life here: new business, new cinema, new music. Things are changing in Scotland.

Today there is a Scottish Parliament in Edinburgh. It is in an interesting new building on the Royal Mile. People from every town and city in Scotland come here to talk about their country. Some Scots want Scotland to speak for itself, in Europe and in the world.

What is in the future for Scotland? Nobody knows. But it is always going to be a beautiful, special place. Perhaps one day you can walk along the Royal Mile, climb the hills, or travel to the islands, and see it for yourself.

Scottish Parliament building

GLOSSARY

also too; as well

bank a building or business for keeping money safely

battle a fight between armies in a war

beach the place where you can walk next to the sea

beat to win a fight or game

become to grow or change, and begin to be something

beef meat from a cow

business buying and selling things; a place where people sell or make things

buy to give money for something

capital (city) the most important city in a country

castle a large, stone building

centre the part in the middle of something

Christian following the teachings of Jesus Christ;
   Christianity *(n)* the religion that follows Jesus Christ

circle a round shape

climb to go up towards the top of something

dance to move your body to music

difficult not easy to do

empty with nothing in or on it

festival a time when a lot of people come together to have fun, make music, dance etc

film a story in pictures that you see at the cinema or on TV

fish farming *(n)* breeding fish as a business

food what you eat

gas something with a strong smell that you burn to make heat

golden eagle a large bird that kills small animals for food

great important or special

grey with a colour like black and white mixed together

gun something that shoots out bullets to kill people

high a long way above the ground

island a piece of land with water around it

kilt a heavy skirt made of tartan

king the most important man in a country

life the time that you are alive; the way that you live

marmalade a soft sweet food made from sugar with oranges or lemons

mountain a very high hill

museum a place where you can look at old or interesting things

music when you sing or play an instrument, you make music; **musician** *(n)* a person who makes music

oats a plant with seeds that are used as food

oil a thick liquid that comes from under the ground, used for energy

parliament the people who make the laws in a country

park a large place with trees and gardens where people can go to walk, play games etc

part one of the pieces of something

place where something or somebody is

poem words written in lines in an artistic way

poor with very little money

queen the most important woman in a country

rock the very hard material that is in the ground

school a place where people go to learn

soldier a person in an army

special not usual or ordinary

sport a game like football, tennis etc

steam engine a machine that uses the power from steam to do things

story words that tell you about what happened in a certain place or time

theatre stories performed by actors

tourist a person who visits a place on holiday

university a place where people study after they leave school

whisky a strong alcoholic drink

world the earth with all its countries and people

Scotland

ACTIVITIES

ACTIVITIES

Before Reading

1 **Match the words to the pictures. You can use a dictionary.**

1 ☐ wall   2 ☐ beach   3 ☐ tartan
4 ☐ island   5 ☐ mountain   6 ☐ castle

2 **You will find eight of these words in the book. Which ones do you think you will find? Why?**

☐ football   ☐ ship   ☐ telephone   ☐ tennis
☐ oil   ☐ party   ☐ ambulance   ☐ drink
☐ guitar   ☐ soldier   ☐ detective   ☐ apples

ACTIVITIES

While Reading

Read Chapter 1, then circle the correct words.

1 Scotland is a country between the *Atlantic / Mediterranean* and the North Sea.

2 Most Scottish people live in the *north / south* of the country.

3 Scotland has about *80 / 800* islands.

4 A person from Scotland is a *Scot / Scotch*.

5 Scottish people are *British / English*.

6 Today everyone in Scotland speaks *Gaelic / English*.

7 In the past, Scotland was *richer / poorer* than it is now.

Read Chapter 2. Match these halves of sentences.

1 The hills of north-west Scotland are . . .

2 People first lived in Scotland . . .

3 The Scottish king Macbeth is famous . . .

4 Mary became queen of Scotland . . .

5 England and Scotland became Great Britain . . .

6 After the Battle of Culloden . . .

a in 1707.

b because Shakespeare wrote about him.

c when she was six days old.

d more than 2,700 million years old.

e many poor families left the Highlands.

f about 9,000 years ago.

Read Chapters 3 and 4, then circle *a*, *b*, or *c*.

1 ____ is the capital city of Scotland.
   a) Glasgow   b) Edinburgh   c) London
2 The ____ Mile goes from Edinburgh Castle to Holyroodhouse.
   a) Royal   b) Old   c) Long
3 Hogmanay is the Scottish name for ____.
   a) Christmas   b) summer   c) 31 December
4 ____ is the biggest city in Scotland.
   a) Edinburgh   b) Birmingham   c) Glasgow
5 In the 1800s, Glasgow started to become rich because people ____ there.
   a) built ships   b) had festivals   c) found oil
6 Glasgow Celtic and Glasgow ____ are football teams.
   a) United   b) Rangers   c) City

Read Chapters 5 and 6. Complete the sentences with the correct places.

Aberdeen / Ben Nevis / Dundee / the Highlands / Inverness / Iona / Lewis / Stirling

1 Boats and planes leave ____ every day for the oil and gas fields of the North Sea.
2 Marmalade from ____ is famous all over the world.
3 A lot of bagpipers come to ____ every September.
4 Mary became queen of Scotland at ____ castle.
5 You can see lochs and hills, and deer and eagles, in ____.
6 ____ is the highest mountain in the United Kingdom.
7 The bodies of many Scottish kings are on ____.
8 There is a 5,000-year-old stone circle on ____.

Read Chapter 7. There is one mistake in each sentence. Write the correct sentences.

1 Golf began in England.
2 Glasgow is the most important place for golf in Scotland.
3 Celtic and Rangers are famous cycling clubs.
4 Between May and September, people meet at the Island Games in more than a hundred different places in Scotland.
5 A kilt needs about two metres of tartan.
6 The Clan Donald families went from Scotland to England about 150 years ago.

Before you read Chapter 8, think about the chapter title, *Five Great Scots*. Do you know any famous people from Scotland? Why are they famous? Are they people from history, or are they still alive?

Read Chapter 8. Answer the questions.

1 Why did Adam Smith go to Rome? How long did he stay there?
2 How old was David Hume when he went to university?
3 Where did Hume meet Voltaire and Rousseau?
4 What do people eat and drink at a Burns Night dinner?
5 When do people sing 'Auld Lang Syne'?
6 What did James Watt like to do when he was a child?
7 What did James Watt and Matthew Boulton make?
8 Which university did Arthur Conan Doyle go to?
9 What was Arthur Conan Doyle's first job?
10 What was the name of Sherlock Holmes's friend?

Read Chapter 9. Are these sentences true (T) or false (F)?

1 People make porridge from vegetables and water.
2 After 1900, many people came to Scotland from Italy and India.
3 Fish farming is very important for Scotland.
4 Gleneagles is a cheap hotel near Perth.
5 Men in some parts of Glasgow have a shorter life than most British men.
6 The word whisky comes from the Gaelic for 'water of the hills'.

Read Chapter 10. Choose the best question word for these questions, and then answer them.

How many / What / Who / Why

1 . . . people live in Scotland?
2 . . . did Alexander Graham Bell make?
3 . . . was the richest man in the world in the 1880s?
4 . . . did David Livingstone go to Africa?
5 . . . did Alan Bean take to the moon in 1969?

Read Chapter 11. Complete the summary with these words.

free, future, love, oil, part, people, Scottish, tartan

The Scots in the USA and Canada ____ the old things, like Scottish dancing and ____. But many of the ____ in Scotland want their country to look to the ____, not the past. Some ____ people do not want Scotland to be ____ of the United Kingdom. They want it to be a ____ country, with a lot of money from ____.

ACTIVITIES

After Reading

1 Here are two postcards from different places in Scotland. Complete them using the words below.

Ben, capital, Castle, eagle, festival, film, Gaelic, highest, Highlands, hill, island, lochs, Mile, Scottish, visitors, west

Hi!
We're staying in Oban, in the ____ of Scotland. Last week we travelled around the ____. We saw some beautiful lakes (the Scots call them ____) and we walked on ____ Nevis, the ____ mountain in the United Kingdom. We saw an ____ high in the sky! Next week we're going to visit Skye, a beautiful ____. Some people there speak ____!
See you! Rico and Marcia

Hello!
We're in Edinburgh! It's the ____ city of Scotland. It's August, and we're enjoying the ____. There are thousands of ____ in the city. There is lots to do. We watched a ____ at the cinema last night. Before that, we walked along the Royal ____ to Edinburgh ____. It's high up on a ____. Tomorrow we're going to hear some ____ music at the Military Tattoo.
Bye! Tina and Joe

2 Use the clues below to complete this crossword with words
   from the story. Then find the hidden nine letter word.

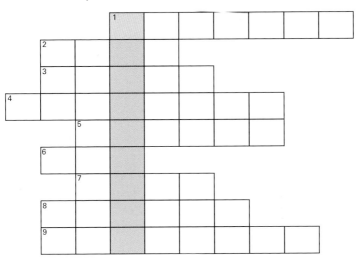

1 Shakespeare wrote about this Scottish king.
2 A _____ is a big, old Scottish family. It has its own tartan.
3 Many Scots people love the poems of Robert _____.
4 The Scots word for the last day of the year, when there is
   a big street party in Edinburgh.
5 Culloden was the last big _____ in Great Britain.
6 This began to bring money into Scotland in the 1970s.
7 Nearly two thousand years ago, the Romans built
   Hadrian's _____ across the most northern part of
   England.
8 Some houses on the Orkney Islands, in the far north of
   Scotland, are the _____ in Europe.
9 Annie Lennox is a musician from _____.

The hidden word in the crossword is _____.
Which city is famous for this food?

3 **Compare Scotland with your country. Use the information in this book.**

You can begin like this:
There are about five million people in Scotland, but in (my country) there are _____ people. People in Scotland speak English, and some people speak Gaelic too. In (my country) people speak _____.

You can write about:
• food and drink
• the weather
• birds and animals
• sports and activities
• things that bring money into the country

4 **Choose a city or part of Scotland that you would like to visit (for example, Edinburgh, Skye, or the Highlands). Find some more information about it, and make a poster or give a talk to your class. Think about these questions:**

• Why would you like to go there?
• What can visitors see and do there?
• What can you find out about its history or its famous people?
• What do people make or do in this part of Scotland?

You can find more information about places to visit in Scotland at www.visitscotland.com and http://en.wikipedia.org/wiki/Scotland.

ABOUT THE AUTHOR

Steve Flinders is a British trainer and writer who has lived and worked in Pakistan, Sweden, Ireland, and France as well as in the UK. He now lives in the beautiful city of York in the north of England and is a director of a training company, York Associates. His wife is French-Italian and they have three grown-up sons. His main job is teaching business people and politicians in York and all over Europe. In his spare time he likes reading, talking politics, going to the theatre, swimming, playing squash badly, and sleeping. His other Oxford Bookworm Factfile title is *The Beautiful Game* (Stage 2).

He is not a Scot but fell in love with Scotland when, at the age of ten, he went on a camping holiday to the island of Colonsay with the Scouts. Since then, he has had many walking holidays there and has climbed many of its best hills. He still believes that Scotland is one of the most beautiful countries in the world – when it's not raining!

OXFORD BOOKWORMS LIBRARY

Classics • Crime & Mystery • Factfiles • Fantasy & Horror
Human Interest • Playscripts • Thriller & Adventure
True Stories • World Stories

The OXFORD BOOKWORMS LIBRARY provides enjoyable reading in English, with a wide range of classic and modern fiction, non-fiction, and plays. It includes original and adapted texts in seven carefully graded language stages, which take learners from beginner to advanced level. An overview is given on the next pages.

All Stage 1 titles are available as audio recordings, as well as over eighty other titles from Starter to Stage 6. All Starters and many titles at Stages 1 to 4 are specially recommended for younger learners. Every Bookworm is illustrated, and Starters and Factfiles have full-colour illustrations.

The OXFORD BOOKWORMS LIBRARY also offers extensive support. Each book contains an introduction to the story, notes about the author, a glossary, and activities. Additional resources include tests and worksheets, and answers for these and for the activities in the books. There is advice on running a class library, using audio recordings, and the many ways of using Oxford Bookworms in reading programmes. Resource materials are available on the website <www.oup.com/bookworms>.

The *Oxford Bookworms Collection* is a series for advanced learners. It consists of volumes of short stories by well-known authors, both classic and modern. Texts are not abridged or adapted in any way, but carefully selected to be accessible to the advanced student.

You can find details and a full list of titles in the *Oxford Bookworms Library Catalogue* and *Oxford English Language Teaching Catalogues*, and on the website <www.oup.com/bookworms>.

THE OXFORD BOOKWORMS LIBRARY
GRADING AND SAMPLE EXTRACTS

STARTER • 250 HEADWORDS

present simple – present continuous – imperative –
can/cannot, must – *going to* (future) – simple gerunds ...

Her phone is ringing – but where is it?

Sally gets out of bed and looks in her bag. No phone. She looks under the bed. No phone. Then she looks behind the door. There is her phone. Sally picks up her phone and answers it. *Sally's Phone*

STAGE 1 • 400 HEADWORDS

... past simple – coordination with *and*, *but*, *or* –
subordination with *before*, *after*, *when*, *because*, *so* ...

I knew him in Persia. He was a famous builder and I worked with him there. For a time I was his friend, but not for long. When he came to Paris, I came after him – I wanted to watch him. He was a very clever, very dangerous man. *The Phantom of the Opera*

STAGE 2 • 700 HEADWORDS

... present perfect – *will* (future) – *(don't) have to, must not, could* –
comparison of adjectives – simple *if* clauses – past continuous –
tag questions – *ask/tell* + infinitive ...

While I was writing these words in my diary, I decided what to do. I must try to escape. I shall try to get down the wall outside. The window is high above the ground, but I have to try. I shall take some of the gold with me – if I escape, perhaps it will be helpful later. *Dracula*

STAGE 3 • 1000 HEADWORDS

... should, may – present perfect continuous   *used to* – past perfect –
causative – relative clauses – indirect statements ...

Of course, it was most important that no one should see Colin, Mary, or Dickon entering the secret garden. So Colin gave orders to the gardeners that they must all keep away from that part of the garden in future. *The Secret Garden*

STAGE 4 • 1400 HEADWORDS

... past perfect continuous – passive (simple forms) –
would conditional clauses – indirect questions –
relatives with *where/when* – gerunds after prepositions/phrases ...

I was glad. Now Hyde could not show his face to the world again. If he did, every honest man in London would be proud to report him to the police. *Dr Jekyll and Mr Hyde*

STAGE 5 • 1800 HEADWORDS

... future continuous – future perfect –
passive (modals, continuous forms) –
would have conditional clauses – modals + perfect infinitive ...

If he had spoken Estella's name, I would have hit him. I was so angry with him, and so depressed about my future, that I could not eat the breakfast. Instead I went straight to the old house. *Great Expectations*

STAGE 6 • 2500 HEADWORDS

... passive (infinitives, gerunds) – advanced modal meanings –
clauses of concession, condition

When I stepped up to the piano, I was confident. It was as if I knew that the prodigy side of me really did exist. And when I started to play, I was so caught up in how lovely I looked that I didn't worry how I would sound. *The Joy Luck Club*

BOOKWORMS · TRUE STORIES · STAGE 1
Mary, Queen of Scots

TIM VICARY

England and Scotland in the 1500s. Two famous queens – Mary, the Catholic Queen of Scots, and Elizabeth I, the Protestant Queen of England. It was an exciting and a dangerous time to be alive, and to be a queen.

Mary was Queen of Scotland when she was one week old. At sixteen, she was also Queen of France. She was tall and beautiful, with red-gold hair. Many men loved her and died for her.

But she also had many enemies – men who said: 'The death of Mary is the life of Elizabeth.'

BOOKWORMS · FACTFILES · STAGE 1
England

JOHN ESCOTT

Twenty-five million people come to England every year, and some never go out of London. But England is full of interesting places to visit and things to do. There are big noisy cities with great shops and theatres, and quiet little villages. You can visit old castles and beautiful churches – or go to festivals with music twenty-four hours a day. You can have an English afternoon tea, walk on long white beaches, watch a great game of football, or visit a country house. Yes, England has something for everybody – what has it got for you?

BOOKWORMS · FACTFILES · STAGE 2
The Beautiful Game
STEVE FLINDERS

Some call it football, some call it soccer, and to others it's 'the beautiful game'. By any name, it's a sport with some fascinating stories. There is murder in Colombia, and a game that lasts for two days where many players never see the ball. There's the French writer who learnt lessons about life from playing football, and the women players who had to leave the club grounds because 'Women's football isn't nice'.

The cups, the leagues, the World Cup finals, the stars, the rules – they're all a part of the world's favourite sport, the beautiful game.

BOOKWORMS · FACTFILES · STAGE 2
Ireland
TIM VICARY

There are many different Irelands. There is the Ireland of peaceful rivers, green fields, and beautiful islands. There is the Ireland of song and dance, pubs and theatres – the country of James Joyce, Bob Geldof, and Riverdance. And there is the Ireland of guns, fighting, death, and the hope of peace. Come with us and visit all of these Irelands – and many more . . .